THE LIFE AND ACHIEVEMENT
OF SUNITA WILLIAMS

Her Remarkable Journey Through
Space and Beyond

LETIS MAUVE

CONTENTS

DEDICATION

To Sunita Williams, whose remarkable journey through space and dedication to scientific exploration continue to inspire future generations.

And to all those who dare to explore the unknown, pushing the limits of human achievement.

INTRODUCTION

Sunita Williams' life story is a reflection of human ambition, scientific exploration, and the unpredictability of space missions. An accomplished NASA astronaut, she has spent her career pushing the boundaries of space travel and expanding humanity's knowledge of life beyond Earth. From her early years of service as a Navy helicopter pilot to setting spaceflight records, Williams' journey reflects a relentless pursuit of progress.

Her accomplishments in space are not just a series of records; they are milestones in a life dedicated to science, exploration, and leadership. But even with her wealth of experience, no one could have anticipated the dramatic turn her 2024 mission would take.

What began as a routine eight-day trip to the International Space Station (ISS) turned into an eight-month nightmare for Williams and fellow astronaut Butch Wilmore. Launched aboard Boeing's Starliner spacecraft, the mission was supposed to be another example of NASA's cutting-edge space programs. Yet, as technical malfunctions plagued the Starliner, their return to Earth became impossible. Stranded on the ISS, Williams and Wilmore faced an extended stay in space, their fates dependent on a rescue mission yet to be planned.

Months of uncertainty followed. With the Boeing Starliner deemed too risky for return, Williams and her crew were left awaiting a solution that finally arrived in the form of a SpaceX Dragon capsule. The rescue mission, led by NASA astronaut Nick Hague and Roscosmos cosmonaut Aleksandr Gorbunov, marked the beginning of the end of their prolonged ordeal in space, bringing a mix of relief and reflection on the fragility of even the most advanced space missions.

This short biography seeks to explore the life of Sunita Williams in a way that intertwines her pioneering career with the broader narrative of space exploration. Her story is one of leadership and an unflinching commitment to science. Whether commanding missions aboard the ISS or facing unexpected challenges in space, Sunita Williams represents the pinnacle of human achievement in the cosmos. As her story unfolds, it becomes a window into both the triumphs and complexities of space travel, reminding us that in the pursuit of progress, the road is often unpredictable.

Science and adventure have shaped her career, and through this biography, readers will journey with her—both on Earth and far beyond.

CHAPTER 1: EARLY LIFE AND EDUCATION

Sunita Williams, a remarkable American astronaut, began her incredible journey on September 19, 1965, in Euclid, Ohio. Born as Sunita Lyn Pandya, she grew up in a family that blended different cultures. Her father, Dr. Deepak Pandya, was an Indian-American neuroanatomist from Gujarat, while her mother, Ursuline Bonnie Pandya, had Slovenian roots. This mix of heritage would later inspire Sunita to carry both Indian and Slovenian symbols into space.

As the youngest of three children, Sunita grew up alongside her older brother Jay Thomas and sister Dina Annad in Needham, Massachusetts. This small town would become the place she considered her true hometown. Her early years were filled with the typical experiences of an American child, but with the added flavor of her diverse background.

Sunita's education began at Needham High School, where she graduated in 1983. Her academic journey then took an exciting turn as she entered the United States Naval Academy in Annapolis, Maryland. Here, she not only pursued her studies but also met her future husband, Michael Williams. In 1987, Sunita earned her Bachelor of Science degree in physical science, setting the stage for her future career in aviation and space exploration.

After graduation, Sunita dove headfirst into her naval career. She began aviator training at the Naval Aviation Training Command in 1987, and by 1989, she was deep into combat helicopter training. Her skills were put to the test during the preparations for the Persian Gulf War in 1990-91, and later during relief missions for Hurricane Andrew in 1992 in Miami, Florida. These experiences shaped her into a skilled and versatile pilot.

In 1993, Sunita's career took another leap forward as she became a naval test pilot. She quickly proved her expertise, eventually becoming a test pilot instructor. Her talent in the cockpit was evident as she gained experience flying more than 30 different aircraft throughout her career.

Continuing her educational pursuits, Sunita earned a Master of Science degree in engineering management from the Florida Institute of Technology in Melbourne in 1995. This additional qualification further prepared her for the challenges that lay ahead in her astronaut career.

The year 1998 marked a significant milestone in Sunita's life as she began her astronaut training. This new chapter led her to Moscow, Russia, where she immersed herself in learning about robotics and other advanced technologies. She worked alongside crews preparing for expeditions to the International Space Station (ISS), gaining invaluable experience that would serve her well in her future space missions.

Throughout her journey, Sunita never forgot her roots. She visited her ancestral village in Gujarat, India, twice in 2007 and 2013, connecting with her heritage and inspiring local students. In Slovenia, her mother's homeland, she became known affectionately as 'Sončka' in the village of Leše, where an astronaut day is celebrated in her honor each September.

Sunita's personal life also flourished alongside her professional achievements. She married Michael J. Williams, a federal police officer based in Texas, and their relationship has spanned over two decades.

Sunita Williams' early life and education laid the foundation for an extraordinary career that would see her set records during her missions to the International Space Station.

CHAPTER 2: MILITARY CAREER

Sunita Williams embarked on her military journey in May 1987, commissioned as an ensign in the U.S. Navy. Her career quickly took flight as she became a Basic Diving Officer after a brief stint at the Naval Coastal System Command. In July 1989, she earned her wings as a Naval Aviator at the Naval Air Training Command, mastering the H-46 Sea Knight helicopter.

Williams' skills were put to the test as she joined Helicopter Combat Support Squadron 8 in Norfolk, Virginia. She ventured across the Mediterranean, Red Sea, and Persian Gulf, participating in Operation Desert Shield and Operation Provide Comfort. Her leadership shone through in September 1992 when she led an H-46 detachment for Hurricane Andrew relief efforts in Miami, Florida, aboard USS Sylvania.

January 1993 marked a new chapter as Williams entered the U.S. Naval Test Pilot School, graduating that December. She then joined the Rotary Wing Aircraft Test Directorate, taking on roles as an H-46 Project Officer and V-22 chase pilot. Her expertise expanded as she flew test flights in various aircraft, including the SH-60B/F, UH-1, and AH-1W.

Williams returned to the Naval Test Pilot School in December 1995, this time as an instructor and Safety Officer. She continued to broaden her flying skills with the UH-60, OH-6, and OH-58. Her naval career reached new heights when she was assigned to USS Saipan as Aircraft Handler and Assistant Air Boss.

In June 1998, while deployed on USS Saipan, Williams' life took an extraordinary turn as NASA selected her for the astronaut program. Throughout her illustrious military career, she logged an impressive 3,000+ flight hours in over 30 different aircraft types, showcasing her exceptional skills and versatility as a naval aviator.

CHAPTER 3: ASTRONAUT CAREER AND SPACEFLIGHT ACHIEVEMENTS

Sunita Williams' journey to becoming an astronaut began in June 1998 when NASA selected her for the astronaut program. At the time, she was deployed on the USS Saipan, serving as the Aircraft Handler and Assistant Air Boss. This selection marked a significant turning point in her career, transitioning from her distinguished naval service to the realm of space exploration.

In August 1998, Williams reported to Johnson Space Center to begin her astronaut candidate training. This intensive program included a wide range of preparation activities. She underwent orientation briefings and tours, attended numerous scientific and technical briefings, and received intensive instruction in shuttle and International Space Station systems. Her training also encompassed physiological preparation and ground school to ready her for T-38 flight training. Additionally, she learned crucial water and wilderness survival techniques, equipping her for various scenarios an astronaut might face.

Following her initial training period, Williams' first assignment took her to Moscow. There, she worked closely with the Russian Space Agency, focusing on their contribution to the space station. She also collaborated with the first Expedition Crew, gaining valuable experience in international space operations.

Sunita Williams' space career has been marked by two significant long-duration missions to the International Space Station (ISS), showcasing her expertise and adaptability in space exploration.

Her first mission, Expedition 14/15, began on December 9, 2006, when she launched aboard the Space Shuttle Discovery as part of the STS-116 mission. Williams served as a Flight Engineer during this expedition. This mission was groundbreaking for Williams, as she established a world record for females with four spacewalks totaling 29 hours and 17 minutes. Her stay on the ISS lasted until June 22, 2007, when she returned to Earth with the STS-117 crew, landing at Edwards Air Force Base in California. This mission lasted a total of 195 days, setting a record for the longest spaceflight by a woman at that time.

Williams' second mission to the ISS, Expedition 32/33, launched on July 14, 2012, from the Baikonur Cosmodrome in Kazakhstan. She traveled alongside Russian Soyuz commander Yuri Malenchenko and Flight Engineer Akihiko Hoshide of the Japan Aerospace Exploration Agency. They were welcomed aboard the ISS on July 17, 2012. During this expedition, Williams took on the role of ISS Commander for Expedition 33, becoming only the second woman to hold this position. This mission also saw Williams participate in three more spacewalks, further adding to her impressive spacewalking record. A unique highlight of this mission was Williams becoming the first person to complete a triathlon in space, coinciding with the Nautica Malibu Triathlon held in Southern California. She creatively used the ISS's equipment to swim, bike, and run in microgravity. Williams and her crew returned to Earth on November 18, 2012, landing in Kazakhstan after spending 127 days in space.

In total, across her two missions, Williams has spent a cumulative 322 days in space, showcasing her endurance and dedication to space exploration.

Sunita Williams' spacewalking achievements stand out as some of the most impressive in the history of space exploration. As of August 2012, she had completed seven spacewalks, totaling an impressive 50 hours and 40 minutes. This accomplishment placed her fifth on the list of most experienced spacewalkers at that time.

During her first mission in 2007, Williams set a world record for females with four spacewalks, accumulating 29 hours and 17 minutes outside the spacecraft. This record was a testament to her skill, endurance, and the trust NASA placed in her abilities to perform critical tasks in the challenging environment of space.

On her second mission, Williams continued to build on her spacewalking expertise. On August 30, 2012, she ventured outside the ISS with JAXA astronaut Akihiko Hoshide to conduct US EVA-18. This spacewalk was particularly significant as they were tasked with removing and replacing the failing Main Bus Switching Unit-1 (MBSU-1) and installing a thermal cover onto Pressurized Mating Adapter-2 (PMA-2). These tasks were crucial for the continued operation and maintenance of the ISS.

Williams' spacewalking achievements went beyond just the number of hours spent outside the spacecraft. Her expertise in performing complex tasks in the unforgiving environment of space contributed significantly to the maintenance and upgrade of the ISS. These spacewalks often involved intricate work with the station's systems, requiring a high level of skill, concentration, and physical endurance.

By the end of her second mission, Williams had once again secured the record for total cumulative spacewalk time by a female astronaut, with 50 hours and 40 minutes. This record stood shows exceptional skills and her crucial role in the ongoing operations of the International Space Station.

Williams' spacewalking achievements not only advanced the objectives of her missions but also inspired future generations of astronauts, particularly women, in the field of space exploration. Her records and accomplishments in this challenging aspect of spaceflight have left an indelible mark on the history of human space exploration.

CHAPTER 4: SCIENTIFIC CONTRIBUTIONS, PERSONAL MILESTONES, AND HONORS

Sunita Lyn Williams has etched her name among the stars - quite literally. Her journey from Earth to space and back again is a tale of determination, courage, and groundbreaking achievements.

As Williams floated in the vast emptiness of space, tethered to the International Space Station (ISS), she wasn't just an astronaut - she was a record-breaker, a pioneer, and an inspiration. During her time on Expedition 14 and 15, Williams set a world record for females with four spacewalks totaling an impressive 29 hours and 17 minutes. Little did she know, this was just the beginning of her spacewalking saga.

But Williams wasn't content with just breaking records in space. In a feat that merged the extraordinary with the ordinary, she became the first person to run a marathon in space. As her feet pounded the treadmill aboard the ISS, her sister Dina Pandya and fellow astronaut Karen L. Nyberg ran the same Boston Marathon on Earth. It was a moment that bridged the gap between the cosmic and the earthly, reminding us that human spirit and determination know no bounds - not even gravity.

Williams' achievements continued to stack up like stars in a constellation. She held the record for the longest single spaceflight by a woman, spending 195 days in space until 2017. Over her career, she accumulated more than 322 days in space, marking her as one of the most experienced female astronauts in history.

But it was during Expedition 32 and 33 that Williams truly cemented her place in the astronaut hall of fame. Launching from the Baikonur

Cosmodrome in Kazakhstan on July 14, 2012, she embarked on a mission that would see her break her own records. During this expedition, Williams performed three more spacewalks, bringing her total to seven. With a cumulative spacewalk time of 50 hours and 40 minutes, she once again held the record for total spacewalk time by a female astronaut.

As if these accomplishments weren't enough, Williams decided to take multitasking to a whole new level - or should we say, a whole new orbit. On September 17, 2012, she became the first person to complete a triathlon in space. Swimming might be tricky in zero gravity, but Williams found a way, using a weightlifting machine to simulate the swimming portion of the race.

Williams' contributions to space exploration have not gone unnoticed. Her trophy cabinet must be as vast as space itself, housing awards such as the Defense Superior Service Medal, the Legion of

Merit, and the NASA Spaceflight Medal. In 2008, she received the Padma Bhushan, India's third-highest civilian award, a testament to her impact not just in America, but across the globe.

But Williams' story isn't just about breaking records and collecting accolades. It's also a tale of cultural pride and personal faith. A devoted Hindu, Williams carried the Bhagavad Gita with her on her space flights, proving that faith can transcend earthly boundaries. Her visits to India, including trips to the Sabarmati Ashram and her ancestral village Jhulasan in Gujarat, highlight her connection to her roots.

In her personal life, Williams is married to Michael J. Williams, a Federal police officer in Oregon. Their shared love for flying helicopters in the early days of their careers shows that the sky was never the limit for this power couple. Williams also has a soft spot for four-legged friends, evident in her pet Jack Russell Terrier, Gorby, who even made a television appearance on the "Dog Whisperer" show.

Williams' journey continues to inspire. In 2015, she was selected for U.S. Commercial space missions, training with Boeing and SpaceX for their commercial crew vehicles. In a historic moment on June 5, 2024, Williams became the first woman to pilot a spacecraft on a flight test for an orbital mission when the Starliner was launched into orbit.

From running marathons in space to piloting groundbreaking spacecraft, Sunita Williams has shown that the sky is not the limit - it's just the beginning. Her story is one of breaking barriers, both on Earth and in space, proving that with determination and courage, humans can achieve the seemingly impossible.

As we look to the future of space exploration, we can be sure that Sunita Williams' legacy will continue to inspire generations of astronauts to come. Her journey reminds us that whether on Earth or among the stars, it's the human spirit that truly allows us to soar.

CHAPTER 5: WILLIAMS' EXTENDED SPACE MISSION AND UNEXPECTED CHALLENGES

Sunita Williams and Butch Wilmore's space adventure took an unexpected turn. What started as an eight-day mission on June 5, 2024, aboard Boeing's Starliner spacecraft, has become an extended stay on the International Space Station. The astronauts, who were supposed to return to Earth after a week, are now scheduled to come back in February 2025 - that's nearly eight months later than planned!

The delay wasn't part of the original plan. The Starliner spacecraft ran into some trouble on its way to the space station. It had problems with helium leaks and some of its thrusters didn't work properly. These issues made NASA worried about bringing the astronauts back safely in the same spacecraft.

NASA and Boeing tried for months to figure out what was wrong and how to fix it. They did tests both in space and on Earth, hoping to find a way to bring Williams and Wilmore home on the Starliner. But in the end, they decided it was too risky.

So, NASA came up with a new plan. Instead of returning on the Starliner, Williams and Wilmore will hitch a ride back to Earth on a SpaceX Crew Dragon spacecraft. SpaceX, the company started by Elon Musk, has been successfully sending astronauts to space for NASA for a while now.

The Starliner won't go to waste, though. It will still return to Earth, but without any astronauts on board. This will give Boeing and NASA a chance to study it and learn from what happened.

Meanwhile, Williams and Wilmore are making the most of their extended stay in space. They're doing scientific experiments, helping maintain the space station, and might even do some spacewalks. It's not the mission they expected, but it's certainly turning into an adventure they'll never forget!

CHAPTER 6: WILLIAMS' INFLUENCE ON WOMEN AND MINORITIES IN STEM

The Indian-American astronaut has become a shining beacon for women and minorities in STEM fields. Her remarkable journey from a "girl next door" to a record-breaking space explorer has inspired countless young minds to reach for the stars.

As a woman in a traditionally male-dominated field, Williams has broken barriers and shattered stereotypes. During her time at the US Naval Academy, she was part of a mere 10% female student body. However, her determination and skills proved that gender is no barrier to success in aerospace. Now, women occupy 20% of seats at the academy, a significant increase that Williams' success has helped foster.

Williams' advocacy for STEM education, particularly for young girls, has been unwavering. She emphasizes that studying STEM today offers a plethora of opportunities to learn, explore, and understand. Her message is clear: nothing is impossible if you're qualified, determined, and willing to make the right decisions.

As a woman of Indian descent, Williams represents the potential for minorities in STEM. She proudly carries her heritage into space, taking samosas and the Bhagavad Gita on her missions. This cultural representation sends a powerful message to minority students that their background is not a hindrance but a strength in the diverse world of science and technology.

Williams' achievements, including her record-breaking spacewalks and her role as the first woman to pilot the Boeing Starliner, serve as tangible proof of what women and minorities can accomplish in STEM. Her story challenges the status quo and encourages underrepresented groups to pursue their passions in science and technology.

Through her numerous public engagements, educational initiatives, and media appearances, Williams continues to inspire the next generation. Her journey from Earth to space and back again shows the power of diversity in advancing human knowledge and exploration.

CONCLUSION

Sunita Williams' career has been defined by her remarkable contributions to space exploration, her role as a leader in NASA, and her ability to overcome the unexpected. From her early days as a Navy helicopter pilot to becoming one of the most experienced astronauts in history, her journey reflects a passion for discovery and an unwavering commitment to scientific progress.

Her achievements in space—the records she set, the groundbreaking missions she commanded—have cemented her place among the great pioneers of human spaceflight. Yet, perhaps one of the most defining moments of her career came not from her numerous successful missions but from the unprecedented challenge she faced in 2024. What was intended to be a routine eight-day trip to the International Space Station became an eight-month ordeal, a reminder of the unpredictable nature of space travel.

Stranded on the ISS with fellow astronaut Butch Wilmore after the failure of Boeing's Starliner spacecraft, Williams' time in space stretched far beyond the original mission. As days turned into weeks, and weeks into months, the weight of uncertainty grew, testing the limits of human endurance. It was a situation no astronaut plans for, yet she confronted it with the same professionalism and strength that had marked her entire career. When the SpaceX Dragon capsule finally arrived to bring her and her crew back to Earth, it was more than a rescue—it was the conclusion of an extraordinary chapter in her life.

Sunita Williams' experiences in space, both planned and unplanned, offer profound insights into the human capacity to adapt, persevere, and achieve greatness in the face of adversity. Her time in space—whether breaking records or enduring an unanticipated eight-month mission—has shown us what it truly means to explore the unknown.

As we look toward the future of space exploration, Williams' legacy will continue to inspire new generations of scientists, astronauts, and explorers. Her story reminds us that while space holds vast potential for discovery, it also presents challenges that test the very core of what it means to be human. Sunita Williams has shown us that no matter how far we venture, the drive to explore, to learn, and to push beyond our limits will always guide us forward.

Made in the USA
Coppell, TX
01 May 2025

48894944R00022